EASY CROCHETING

PERFECT CROCHET PATTERNS FOR BEGINNERS

JAMIE J.

CONTENTS

Introduction	1
How to Crochet	2
Holding a Crochet Hook	4
How to Stitch	7
Crocheting Fabric	9
Types of Crocheting	11
The Finishing	14
Different Stitches	17
More Crocheting Styles	20
Afghan Patterns	22
Sneak Peek - Chapter 1	26

©Copyright 2022 – **All rights reserved by Jamie J.**

The content of this book may not be reproduced, duplicated, or transmitted without direct written permission from the author or publisher.

ISBN: 978-1-63970-141-4

Legal Notice:

This book is copyright protected. This is only for personal use. You cannot amend, distribute, sell, use, quote, or paraphrase any part of the content within this book without the consent of the author or publisher.

Disclaimer notice:

Please note the information contained within this document is for educational and entertainment purposes only.

Every attempt has been made to provide accurate, up-to-date, and reliable complete information.

No warranties of any kind are expressed or implied. Readers acknowledge that the author is not engaging in the rendering of legal, financial, medical or professional advice. The content of this book has been derived from various sources. Please consult a licensed professional before attempting any techniques outlined in this book.

By reading this document, the reader agrees that under no circumstances is the author responsible for any losses, direct or indirect, which are incurred as a result of the use of the information contained within this document, including, but not limited to, -errors, omissions, or inaccuracies.

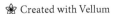 Created with Vellum

INTRODUCTION

Crocheting has become an important art, and therefore there is a great need for people to know how to do it.

Every time a person looks at a blanket, little emphasis is paid to its production process. Crocheting is, therefore, the art of making garments by use of a hooked needle.

By reading this book, I hope you will glean some nuggets out of it and become an expert in crocheting. Welcome abroad to this crocheting journey and enjoy yourself.

HOW TO CROCHET

Talking Point 1: Meaning of Crocheting

Crocheting is the art of making garments by use of a hooked needle. This hooked needle is therefore referred to as crochet. In essence, this process involves interlocking and looping of thread, yarn, or fiber strands to create.

Talking Point 2: Role of Crocheting in Society

As an integral part of humanity, this seemingly magical undertaking of using a single hook and strands of yarn to make garments cannot be overemphasized. One needs to look at mats, blankets, and pullovers to see their importance. In modern times, interests have emerged, with many people making a career out of it. This resolve in many people has been ignited by the pleasure of producing high-quality yarn items and the financial rewards. End crocheted products are determined by what crochet hooks one uses and the artistry of the crocheter. Therefore, in making clothes, big hooks made of aluminum are predominant, while dollies are made of fine steel hooks. Items like mats may be made using big wooden or plastic hooks.

. . .

Talking Point 3: The Crocheting Hook

It is suitable for beginners to know that most hooks are six inches long and are alphabetically classified. The classifications range from B, which is the smallest, to Q, which is the largest. Creativity bestows the honor of crocheting to the hook, without which there can never be crocheting. A casual look at a crochet hook reveals a piece of art that bends into a hook at the end. But a keener look shows different parts to this seemingly simple tool.

One end meticulously has a hook which is used with the yarn to make stitches or loops. On the other end is the throat, whose role is to aid a crocheter in sliding the stitch on the working area of the crochet hook. Just about the middle is the thumb rest, also known as the finger hold. It has a flat design which makes gripping of the hook with the thumb and third finger easy. And finally, we have the crochet's handle. Technically, it is supposed to rest under a crocheter's fourth and fifth fingers. It helps create a balance in this multi-tasking art which involves the fingers, the yarn, and the hook.

Article I.DIY Learn How to Crochet Hook Case Holder Folder Wallet-Storage for Hooks:

https://www.youtube.com/watch?v=3gho3ZHKnZo&spfreload=10

HOLDING A CROCHET HOOK

Talking Point 1: How to hold a Crochet

Crocheting is an art, just like playing the guitar, and one should find a way of using the hook. However, getting acquainted with a hook is a personal initiative perfected through constant use by the beginner.

Examples abound that would help a beginner know how to use a hook. The knife method or over-the-hook method is an excellent example of learning how to hold and work with a hook. A beginner should therefore demystify working with a hook by visualizing the everyday act of holding a knife. The beginner's hand should grip over the crochet hook as the first step. Then the handle should rest against the palm of one's hand. The thumb and third finger should grip the thumb rest. In summary, one should hold the crochet hook the same way one holds a knife while cutting meat. Therefore, the rule is to make sure the thumb and middle finger are holding the thumb-rest and the crochet hook's handle is resting against one's palm.

The pencil or fork method, also called the under-the-hook method, is another illustration of using the hook. The way a pencil is held should also help the beginner get accustomed to holding a crochet hook. Here, the beginner should hold the hook like a pencil with his thumb while the index finger should rest on the finger hold. The third finger should be placed near the tip of the hook.

The beginner should turn the crochet hook slightly towards one's posture but should be careful not to face it up or down. Holding the crochet hook firmly but not tightly should be ingrained in the beginner's mind. Exercise is the mother of perfection, and with time one overcomes the fear of gripping the crochet hook tightly.

A beginner should hold the crochet hook just as it goes when a person holds a fork while eating. The thumb and forefinger should grip the thumb-rest, while the handle should rest on the fleshy area of the forefinger. Back to Basics Crochet: Holding the Hook, Yarn tension, and Slip Knot:

https://www.youtube.com/watch?v=pgFD4P5s-NA

Talking Point 2: How to Hold Yarn for a Crochet

There are no rules on holding the yarn for the crochet. But there is an unwritten rule where the yarn is put on the beginner's less active hand. The hand holding the yarn works in unison with the left hand in feeding the yarn to the crochet. It is therefore paramount for a beginner to work out their style. One should note that the yarn hand controls the tension of the yarn being fed to the crochet hook, which finally determines how tight or loose one's finished project will be. Beginning Crochet: How to Hold the Yarn and Crochet Hook:

https://www.youtube.com/watch?v=YvdfdkaL1Qw

Talking Point 3: Making a Crochet Slipknot

Like with every other venture in life, crocheting begins with a foundation chain called beginning or a series of stitches. Every crochet project begins with a slip knot. A beginner starts by making a slip knot on the crochet hook with 5 to 6 inches of the free end of the yarn for training purposes. The string of a yarn should be held in the beginner's left hand. Then by grasping a crochet hook in the right hand, the crochet should be put between the middle finger and thumb while the index finger should rest near the tip of the hook. Sliding a piece of yarn through the first loop, the beginner takes the crocheting needle and puts it through the loop without letting go of the end. To bring the yarn's tail end, one must push it through to make a loop. Finally, one has a nice loop on the crocheting needle. The emphasis is to practice hard to grasp the essential details of holding the yarn with the left hand for easy crocheting. How to Make a Crochet Slip Knot: Beginner Crochet:

https://www.youtube.com/watch?v=w9wEcSD-V3M

HOW TO STITCH

Talking Point 1: The Art of Stitching

The Stitches should be created on the crochet's working area. One should avoid the throat when making stitches. This caution is premised because using the throat tightens the stitches, unlike stitches on the finger hold, which tends to relax and stretch the stitch. Though the thickness of yarn or thread and the size of the hook determine the quality of the product, again the mastery by the crocheter is vital in determining the quality of the product. The experience in manipulating the crochet can birth a variety of different quality products. How to Crochet: Single Crochet Stitch (Beginners):

https://www.youtube.com/watch?v=BCDA44Sijx4

Talking Point 2: Most Appropriate Crochet Hook

As said earlier, the hook is the cornerstone. For beginners, a size H-8 is the most popular, but crocheting specialists recommend I-9 hook. Crochet I-9 creates bigger stitches, and it is user-friendly. Beginners should also shun the use of wooden or plastic hooks. The underlying disadvantage is that the yarn does not smoothly glide over these wooden or plastic hook surfaces. But to the well-versed crocheters, these types of hooks are magnificent. Therefore, an aluminum hook is the most preferred hook for beginners since it is easier to use and pocket-friendly. Crochet Yarn, Hook Sizes-What works Best:

https://www.youtube.com/watch?v=zFTylXH3BZY

Talking Point 3: Yarn and a Pair of Scissors

Just Just as vital as crochet is to crochet, so also the correct yarn supply. The yarn color is a critical ingredient because an appealing and enchanting color that is food for the eye. Multicolored yarn should be given a wide berth because its stitches will be exceedingly difficult to distinguish by a beginner of crocheting. On the other hand, bright colors make the stitches distinguishable, and the beginner's progress is vividly seen. The worsted fabric of acrylic or fibers made of wool is preferred because they have a hard textured surface with no nap. Nap is the yarn that stands up from the weave, as one would see in a velvet, rug, or corduroy. But this should not be a rule of thumb because the cost implications must also be factored in.

A pair of small sharp-pointed scissors should be part of the crocheting tools. This pair of scissors comes in handy, particularly when cutting the yarn. Types of Crochet Yarn ad their Different Uses: Crochet Yarn

https://www.youtube.com/watch?v=6979knxSLKM

CROCHETING FABRIC

Talking Point1: Shaping of Yarn

Crocheted fabric is done by placing a slip-knot loop on the hook. Pulling one more loop through the first loop and continuously redoing the process creates a chain of a suitable length. The chain is further turned and worked in rows. More action is incorporated when the chain is joined to the beginning of the row with a slip stitch and worked in rounds. Other rounds can also be created by working many stitches into a single loop. Stitches are made by pulling one or more loops through each loop of the chain. At any one time at the end of a stitch, there is only one loop left on the hook. The Art of Sock making with Red Heart Yarns:

https://www.youtube.com/watch?v=tVkZ85drobs

Talking Point 2: The Pretzel Technique

It is a technique where the yarn is shaped into a pretzel (glazed and salted cracker typically in the shape of a loose knot) before making your crochet slip knot. First, one takes the tail end of the yarn and loops it over the working end of yarn. Next, by pulling and folding the tail end of the yarn towards the back of the loop, a pretzel shape is made. Finally, the hook is inserted through the first loop of the pretzel so that when the loop is pulled through , a crochet slip knot is made. How to Tie a Man's Scarf the Pretzel Knot:

https://www.youtube.com/watch?v=_OOVvmzpi7E

Talking Point 3: The "X" and Flip Techniques

In this technique, the yarn is shaped into an X shape before making the slip knot. Here, the tail end of yarn is taken and wrapped around the middle and index fingers. A letter X is formed when a beginner crosses the tail end of yarn over the top of the fingers. By pushing yarn through the first loop, the beginner should be careful not to push it too far while causing the entire tail end to come through. The process continues by pulling the index and middle fingers out of the X loop and grabbing the working and tail end of yarn hence tightening it to create a crochet slip knot.

This technique involves taking the tail end of the yarn and looping it over the working end of the yarn. This process is carried out by holding the yarn or laying it on a flat surface. The beginner pulls over the loop and flips it over the working end of the yarn. The hook is placed in the dominant hand and slid under the working strand of yarn under the loop. The beginner pulls the working end of the yarn through the loop with the crochet hook, and finally, a slip knot is created. DIY Learn How to Crochet-Flip Flop Sandals Shoes, Beach with Beads, Ruffle Yarn Pom, Yarn and Fur:

https://www.youtube.com/watch?v=T_Rz2MXc6-Y

TYPES OF CROCHETING

Talking Point 1: Learn the Crochet Chain

In crocheting, the chain stitch is the foundation stitch and is used at the starting of projects. Therefore, beginners must master the crochet chain, knowing that most patterns begin with a chain stitch. Little wonder, it is known as a foundation chain. The beginner should make a slip knot and then place it on the hook. When five or seven loops are drawn one through the other and joined to the center stitch of the preceding row, we refer this to the crochet chain or the open-chain crochet, and it is used to make purses.

With the crochet chain (foundation chain) getting longer, the beginner should continue to move the fingers up the chain and keep control. It is worth noting that each chain should be the same size while ensuring the yarn's tension is the same. As said earlier, one should adjust the stitches tight or relaxed if one cannot pull the hook through the stitch by relaxing the hands or making the grip tighter. It is vital to count the chain stitches after finishing the chain to know how many have been made. Procedurally, the beginner should count the first stitch that is right underneath the loop on the hook

When one has finished the chain, one may not be sure how

many chain stitches have been created. To therefore begin by counting the first stitch that is right underneath the loop on your hook. While counting the stitches, the beginner should never count the loop that is still on the hook. More to it, the slip knot should never be counted. Simple Crochet-How to Make the Crochet Chain Beginner Stitches:

https://www.youtube.com/watch?v=NelL5hJ1mfQ

Talking Point 2: The Slip Stitch
As said earlier, stitching is the backbone of crocheting, so these are the main stitches. You can work a slip stitch at just about any point after you have begun your project. If you already have an active loop on your crochet hook, insert your hook into the spot where you want to crochet the slip stitch. Then hook your yarn, pull the yarn up through both your project and the active loop on your hook. The slip stitch is now complete. #12 How to Slip Stitch: Beginner Crochet:

https://www.youtube.com/watch?v=AFk-fdAowbY

Talking Point 3: The Single Crochet
To make a chain of about twenty chain stitches, the beginner should hold the chain in the left hand. Then the beginner slips the hook into the second loop in the chain. Then grab the yarn with the hook and pull it through the loop. Already two loops have been made on the crocheting needle. With the two loops on the crocheting needle, reach over and grab the yarn again through both loops.

Upon pulling the yarn through both loops, the beginner will have one loop on the needle again. What the beginner has just made is what is called single crochet. By repeating this process as above in the next loop on the chain, the beginner should continue to work one single crochet into each chain until she reaches the end of the row. The beginner should remember to keep the hook in the right

hand and turn what she has crocheted over. When done, the crochet needle is removed by pulling on the yarn, which comes out on its own; when one has mastered making the single crochet stitch, products like a crocheted rug or a potholder.

It's good for beginners to remember that the smallest stitch used in crocheting is the single crochet. Its advantages are that it gives a closely woven fabric that is firm and with a pretty seeded and attractive fine or bulky yarn. Extra chains are made at the onset of working on any crochet stitches. This make is vital for it brings the hook up to the same height as the stitch being worked while giving the fabric a straight edge.#6 How to Single Crochet Stitch: Beginner Crochet:

https://www.youtube.com/watch?v=wgVOkQcf5qw

THE FINISHING

Talking Point1: Finished Crochet Works

Like in every profitable venture, the drive is to finish crochet projects. A look at the final products reveals attractive, beneficial, and good-looking. Some of the most loved and popular products include Afghans, baby blankets, hats, scarves, shawls, and purses, among many others, with the mastery of crocheting, complex products that will include curtains, jewelry, and socks. When uncoiled into its basic loop, a hank of wool yarn can be wound into a ball for crocheting, unlike crocheting from a normal hank directly tangles the yarn and produces snarls. This is a reminder to the crocheter of the importance of working with proper yarn. Crochet 101 Finish Off:

https://www.youtube.com/watch?v=RCTwwyQF298

Finishing Your Crochet Project: https://www.youtube.com/watch?v=KcXiX5zYKto

. . .

Talking Point 2: How to Change Color in Crochet

Challenges abound when changing color at the onset or end of a row. One is always tempted never to complete the last stitch but desires to continue working to the previous stitch to the last two loops on hook. So, to overcome the challenge, a beginner can fold the new yarn color in half by leaving 4 to 5 inches of yarn on the tail end. Then she should pinch the two ends together at the top by using the thumb and index finger. Placing the new yarn on the hook and pulling the new color through the two loops on your hook suffices. From there, the beginner should cut the first color's attached strand of yarn, leaving 4 to 5 inches of yarn attached. Then pull on both the old and new tail ends and loose strands of yarn to secure the new color into place.

The process further includes turning the piece workaround and holding the loose strands together at the back of the piece. Crocheting over the two loose strands 4 to 6 times before cutting the loose strands with your scissors is what follows. A repetition of the process brings out the changed color.

Correct Way to Change Yarn Color in Crochet: Beginner Crochet

https://www.youtube.com/watch?v=6979knxSLKM

Talking Point 3: How to Finish a Crochet

The beauty of every crocheted project is leaving enough yarn at the end to allow weaving in or a finish. The finished project is what gives way to the first cut. The beginner must make sure that she leaves at least 4 to 6 inches of yarn onto a weaved project. Using the small pair of scissors, you are supposed to cut. Not cutting the 4-6 inches of yarn after causes poor finishing and strands pop out and closing the weave is never realized and this compromises the quality of the product. Remember the 4-6 yarn is used in weaving at the end of a project by crochet hook. Dip

the Yarn in the last loop that is on your hook. Pull the yarn strand tight with your fingers, and that is all there is to this lesson. Use the crochet hook to pull the loose end of yarn through the last loop on the hook. This way, the product looks spectacular.
Finishing Your Crochet Project

https://www.youtube.com/watch?v=pz2UC_RvNs0

DIFFERENT STITCHES

Talking Point 1: Double Crochet Stitch

Double crochet is done by following the same path as in the single crochet stitch the difference comes by omitting the one-loop stitch and working until the beginner has made two long stitches between each of the long ones. It is the second most popular crochet stitch.

The double crochet stitch consists of two single crochet stitches in height. But again, it is not as tight as the single crochet stitch. One can tell the beauty of the stitch by looking at blankets, scarves, and sweaters, which are made using this double crochet stitch.

https://www.youtube.com/watch?v=5xKssKskNzo

Talking point 2: Foundation Chain

It is good to note that when a beginner starts a crochet project using a foundation chain, one is always tempted to place the first double crochet into the fourth chain from the hook. One should always enter the hook into the top loop of the chain unless the pattern one uses requires a different addition, but the procedure involves putting the yarn over the hook, which is followed by pulling or drawing the yarn through the chain. Note that there now will be three loops on hook. Yarn over the hook and pull the yarn through only the first two loops on hook and not through the last loop. Here, the first two loops become part of the stitch, leaving the newly created loop on the hook and the last loop that one didn't pull the yarn through. By now, there will now be two loops on your hook and continue to yarn over the hook. Pull the yarn through the last two loops on your hook, and your first double crochet is now complete. Now finish placing all your double crochets into the foundation chain.

https://www.youtube.com/watch?v=5xKssKskNzo

Talking Point 3: Double Crochet - Second Row

On double crocheting on the second row, chain3, and turn your workaround. When double crocheting, the beginner will always want to chain 3 when moving up a row. Remember that chain three counts as your first double crochet and is also considered the turning chain. Yarn over the hook and insert the hook into the second stitch, not the first stitch when double crocheting into your second row and all of the rows that follow, and you will always want to skip the first stitch and place your first double crochet into the second stitch. Then the turning chain counts as your first double crochet. The stitch that you will be working in is made up of two strands of yarn. The stitch looks like the letter V. Yarn over the hook. Pull or draw the yarn through the stitch. There will now be three loops on your hook. Repeat steps 5 through 8 from the first row. The only difference is that you will be crocheting into the double crochet stitch rather than the foundation chain. When finishing your rows, remember to work your last double crochet stitch into the turning chain.

How to Double Crochet Stitch: Beginner Crochet:

https://www.youtube.com/watch?v=5xKssKskNzo

MORE CROCHETING STYLES

Talking Point 1: Half Double Crocheting

This half-double crochet is a stitch that can be learned with ease—primarily used in the making of hats and headbands because it is a closely fitting stitch. When placing the half double stitch into the foundation chain, the beginner will always want to place this stitch into the third chain from the hook. So the crocheted ends up with the original two loops over the hook with the third loop from the chain. It is good to enter the hook into the top loop of the chain unless the pattern one is using requires something different. Yarn over the hook and draw the yarn through the chain. The beginner now has three loops on the hook. This way, the beginner will have completed her first half double stitch.

How to Do a Half Double Stitch

https://www.youtube.com/watch?v=2uG5Tc-C0u4

Talking Point 2: Triple or Treble Crochet Stitch

This stitch is also called the triple crochet stitch or the treble crochet stitch. While stitching, the beginner should remember to make the long stitches upon the loops and the loops on the preceding long stitches. The learner should increase by going twice in the same loop and decrease by missing one loop.

How to Crochet- The triple/Treble Crochet Stitch(TR): https://www.youtube.com/watch?v=FSPJhog9lL4

Talking Point 3: Advanced Stitching

When triple crocheting, one will always want to do chain four counts when moving up a row. The chain four counts as your first triple crochet stitch, which is also called the turning chain. The learner should continue by yarning over the hook twice and placing the hook into the second stitch. It is also good for the learner to remember that she already has the first stitch since she had chained earlier. This stitch which looks like the letter V is what the learner is working with and consists of two strands of yarn. In this kind of stitching, triple crochet is commonly used for less straining crochet projects. It is known to produce a looser, see-through type effect and more so used for loose sweaters, shawls, and scarves.

Advanced Cross Stitch Skills:

https://www.youtube.com/watch?v=78CmJ2MRjCc

AFGHAN PATTERNS

In the crocheting world, the Afghan patterns hold a pivotal place. They come in different shapes and sizes. From the Afghans crocheting, you will get assorted and granny squares as products. Other designs include children, floral, and baby products.

Talking Point 1: Crocheting Afghan Patterns

For beginners in crocheting, one may think they are walking a tightrope by tackling this project. It is, therefore, for a beginner to experiment with these patterns. The best one for beginners is the use of the granny square. This method will note that the squares have been worked as individual pieces, and one can only have sewn them up. The joy with afghan patterns is that they are beginner-friendly, and one should not shy away from it.

Basic Crocheting Rules

It is always worth noting that when working with the loops, it is mandatory to crochet by way of the top of the stitching. But there is an exception if the guidelines of the pattern have been provided. That way, one has to follow these instructions.

. . .

What is closest to your face is what is termed as the Front Loop. What is farther away from you is what is termed as Back Loop. When the back or front of a stitch is worked, we refer to this post as the "stem".

Reach to the height of the worked stitches turning chains is what is applied. In their absence, crochet begins to bend at the edges. The length of a stitch is what determines the size of the chain.

Talking Point Two: Crochet Additions

Finger Crochet Necklace

You need not have been a crocheter or a top-notch designer to create this necklace. All you require is yarn and a knack for creativity to make this necklace. In terms of skills in crocheting, nothing much is expected but only use of the hands.

Materials

Purple Haze

Hank

A color that you love

The necklace should be forty-four inches or 112 centimeters long.

Instructions

Start by unwinding the yarn as you fold in half the whole length of yarn. Move on by making a slip knot that should be loose by using the yarn's double-length. It should be about thirty-eight centimeters or fifteen inches. You have created a large loop from this yarn.

The slip knot should be held by one hand. You should make sure that the index finger and the thumb of the opposite hand loop over your slip knot. Take the yarn that you doubled and produced a new loop. It is a process termed finger crocheting. But one can still use different fingers, and so it should not be an inhibitor. The process of making new loops should not cease until the yarn that has been crocheted elongates to 38 centimeters or fifteen inches which go beyond the knot. You have now come to the finish line of the knot of the yarn and, finally, trim it.

But this is not the rule of the thumb since crocheters are endowed differently, so room for diversity is allowed.

Talking Point 3: Imagine Scarf

The role of the scarf is to keep one warm when temperatures dip. An Imagine Scarf is the delight of so many people in the world due to its appealing design. It is recommended as a project for all beginners since it is not complicated in its conception.

Materials

Brown sugar one hank

Color that appeals to one.

One should not be obsessed with the gauge of the crochet. Instead, one should move the hand to the yarn tube's end. The other side should hold the highest part of the yarn tube and finally pull it down. The process should continue until both ends meet, then ends should be held firmly as the tube is slid through one's arm and you have now created a yarn's double layer and, therefore, the imagined scarf.

Butterfly Scarf

Handmade shawls are classy with appealing patterns any day, any time. They appeal across the board whether one is in a T-shirt or is dressed formally.

. . .

Purple Haze one Hank

Strawberry fields one spiral
   Colors that appeal to you
   Crochet hook G-6
   Large-eyed needle(blunt)

It should be about 167.5 (which is 66 inches) centimeters and elongate along the edges. In creating the shawl, the length of A and B must be crocheted with the one's choice of colors. The colors to use here are Magenta and Dark Purple.

The End.

Did you like this book? Then you'll LOVE Essential Massage Oils: The Ultimate Guide On The Use Of Oils

Essential Oils are derivatives from natural sources, and these are entirely plant-related i.e. taken from kernels, rinds, flowers, seeds, and even plant parts like the bark and roots. They have therapeutic and relaxing effects when applied to the skin or just inhaled. As they are plant derivatives, Essential Oils play a vital role in perfumery and even in food processing as aromatic enhancers.

Essential Massage Oils: The Ultimate Guide On The Use Of Oils

https://books2read.com/u/3yK6O6

SNEAK PEEK - CHAPTER 1

Essential Massage Oils: The Ultimate Guide On The Use Of Oils

https://books2read.com/u/3yK6O6

Usage and Application Guide

Essential Oils are potent owing to their concentrated nature. And understanding the application and usage is quite important. This does not mean that you must take overwhelming classes to be able to use them. Just follow these essential tips that have been specially compiled for you. A thing to note here is that Essential Oils have different properties and should not use all oils the same way or for various purposes. These tips are aimed at the novice and the regular user to keep a handy note to refer. And see how to use these oils for your wellbeing and the people around you.

. . .

Personal Judgment: When it comes to tools to better understand Essential Oils, the best one and the foremost one is your nose. Your mind and intuitions play a vital role in what you use for your body, and this can take you long in the ever-widening route of knowledge. Once you know what is good for you, experiment with other oils.

Start Small: An excess of anything is harmful. The oils that we use are very potent and may be detrimental if not used wisely. If you feel confused about using new oil, read the precautions, consult a doctor, apply a small amount as a patch test and finally use the oil after diluting it to a good extend.

Reading the Label: Usually, Essential Oils come with a colored code in the label:

Green: Is generally safe for use and can be used undiluted

Orange: Safe for general use and can be used diluted moderately.

Red: Heavy dilution is required and also to consult a doctor before use.

Though the green and orange are safe, wise discretion and a doctor's advice are always better.

All Oils are Different:

. . .

Oils like Peppermint and Lemon have diverse uses in the application. But some are Topical Oils like Eucalyptus and cannot take this internally.

While it is always wise to follow precautions, a general rule is that only well-known brands publish precautions based on actual research. Brands that are cheap and not well known may not produce precautions based on research, and they also may have a lot of contaminants in them. Therefore, when using oil internally, it should take great care, and it always is better to do so under a prescription from a reputed practitioner.

HOW TOS ON ESSENTIAL OILS:

Aromatic Uses of Essential Oils:

The most common and widely used application of Essential Oils is Aromatic. They smell delicious, and so the widespread use of it aromatically. They also stimulate the Limbic System, which is responsible for the moods that often come and go. Some oils also rid us of nasal congestions.

Aromatic properties can:

Improve indoor air purity, prevent many airborne diseases, and even detoxify some of the contaminants.

Improve mood, balance hormones, and provide for emotional and spiritual well-being.

. . .

Be a complete cure for the sinuses and respiratory system.

Improve the immune system and benefit overall health.

Essential Oils are volatile, and when massaging onto the body, the fumes arising from them get to you internally through your respiratory system.

The fumes contain thousands of beneficial compounds present in the parent oil and can infuse the effects deeply into your system. The nasal sensations directly affect the Limbic system and can enhance or relax your mood.
End of Sneak Peek.

Essential Massage Oils: The Ultimate Guide On The Use Of Oils

https://books2read.com/u/3yK6O6

©Copyright 2022 by Jamie J.
All rights Reserved

In no way is it legal to reproduce, duplicate, or transmit any part of this document in either electronic means or in printed format. Recording of this publication is strictly prohibited and any storage of this document is not allowed unless with written permission from the publisher. All rights are reserved. Respective authors own all copyrights not held by the publisher.

❦ Created with Vellum

www.ingramcontent.com/pod-product-compliance
Lightning Source LLC
Chambersburg PA
CBHW052314090225
21681CB00011B/1071